THE DARKLIGHT SERIES

~ BOOK II ~

SHADOWS & SCARS

T. JASON VANDERLAAN

BALM AND BLADE
PUBLISHING

ISBN: 978-0-9841386-6-1

Published by Balm and Blade Publishing
1927 Mountain Road
Hamburg, PA 19526
www.balmandblade.com

Cover design by Matthew J. Lucio and T. Jason Vanderlaan

For those who saw the Promised Land
and welcomed it from a distance.

Contents

III. The Soil From Which I've Grown

IV. Now You Can Pretend Like You Knew Me All Along

V. Detours & Detox

VI. Goodbyes, Farewells, and Other Beginnings

VII. Shelter

Prelude

More than anything,
I am afraid to be known.

Haunted by the fear
that I will never be seen
for who I really am inside –
the good and the bad –
and loved anyway.

Sometimes I hide,
unwilling to offer, reluctant to trust;
but the longing always draws me out,
beckons me to keep searching,
to risk everything for a chance
to find this love.

Because more than anything else,
I want to be known.

I.

Even Now, We're at Odds

Unbidden

I swear I've said goodbye to you
more times than you ever said
you loved me.

I can't seem to get you
to leave for good:

I keep finding you,
unbidden, haunting my dreams
without warning, without reason –

your slow-motion hair floating around my face,
irresistible fingers caressing,
soft warmth around the back of my neck
as you pull me close.

Your lips, curving into satisfaction,
coming closer, closer,
just close enough to whisper:
I don't want you anymore.

Escaping October

You're not the only one
who's changed.

I've changed too –
the color of fall leaves,
the shape of fallen raindrops
on a dreary day in October.

You're not the only one
who's stayed the same.

I've stayed the same too –
a stark, barren tree,
an overcast sky
on an bleak day in October.

You're not the only one
who feels trapped.

No one ever said
this had to be permanent,
but I fear we will never escape
this endless day in October.

What We Wanted

Your love is the broken-handled ax
that failed me as the winter storms rolled in.
Fire burned to coal, cooled to ash,
and nothing remained to be given.

The ice on my eyes only stings a little,
but at least you're not here
to freeze with me.

I am the parched canteen
that failed you as the desert sun rose high.
You drank from my depths and found
I was everything you never wanted.

The sweat in your eyes may sting a little,
but at least I'm not there
to burn with you.

Strangers

Do you remember when
this was easy?

I love you meant just that.
I could take your hand
and save the day.

Now we are
standing, hands in our pockets,
staring at the strangers passing by.

Do you remember when
this was simple?

No reason needed
to escape the madding crowd – enough
just to be near each other.

Now we are
standing, hearts in our chests,
staring at the strangers we've become.

Bullet

Time has a way
of moving like the tides –
washing in and over and out
while we stand stationary.

As we watch,
the world around us changes,
even as we do.

I want you to know
I'd still take a bullet for you
or for the one you love.

And time has a way
of rushing like a flood –
carving out a canyon
deep and wide and deserted.

We wait and watch
as a chasm grows
between our hearts.

I want you to know
I'd still take a bullet for you
even if it came from your gun.

T. Jason Vanderlaan

This Void is All the Proof I Need

I dare say
as I tilt the glass back,
I am just as eager
as when I first filled it.

I will drink it all,
every last drop,
knowing that I loved
just as much
as the glass is now empty.

You were my first,
my last regret.

The Passive Voice is Weak

I'm always the passive one,
even in my poetry,
the one place I have control.

I stand, paralyzed, as you

stab,
twist,
laugh.

Maybe this is inescapably me,
but I'm taking a chance it's not.

I grab your wrist
and squeeze until you drop
the knife, your smile.

I'm sorry if it hurts,
but you were killing me.

T. Jason Vanderlaan

Sandcastles at High Tide

I.
On the threshold, you stand
casually ignorant of the way
I still let you inside.

Even from this distance
I can tell your voice is cold.

II.
I offer an exchange:
painted smiles,
honest tears.

III.
We'll try to rest in peace
and not disturb the flowers,
but there are some things
even the dead must say.

We're just reliant little princes
singing about mood rings
and flowers with four small thorns.

IV.
You never knew
how much I loved,
but I always knew
I'd never be enough.

12

V.
Her words:
sharp as thorns,
soft as rose petals;

water to cleanse the cut,
and salt to make it sting.

VI.
Let me dream this dream away
and forget what will never be.

The Death of a Friend

I don't believe in ghosts,
but I swear only a ghost of you remains,
though you walk among the living
like you have a reason to stay.

I used to think
you had changed,
but now I'm afraid
you have passed away.

If you need to hear it from me:
Rest in peace, dear friend.
I hope you find comfort
in your return to clay.

End Cycle

You cut yourself free
only to be entangled again,
and I have nothing left to offer
but fire for frayed ends.

I guess I have my own hang-ups,
my own one-track mind.

I want to derail –
too long pursuing this pain
with nothing left to gain.

No resolution to wrestling
with the anger and the ache –
two sides of the same coin,
perpetually spinning, flipping,
falling without a place to land.

No option left except to end this
the same way it began:
with a step into the unknown.

Only this time, my hands will be empty.

Everything I Had to Offer

In love for the first time,
I found myself
with you by my side.

You saw me
as more myself
than anyone before,

and you left.

Good Mourning, Good Knight

You said I had come true, come through
with my shining armor (now dulled,
rusted, broken by your absence,
by the falling of my tears).

I know I crushed you
with my insecurities,
but I think we weren't so different;
we just hid behind different disguises.

I can't say who's to blame:
you for not letting me in,
or me for not getting through,

but I know I still feel
the weight of your disappointment,
the weight of you walking away from me.

I hope you found your knight.
I hope you let him in.

II.

Desert Wells & Mirages

The Wanderer: Desert Promises

Maybe it was the emptiness. As far as the eye could see: nothing but sand. And him. Even in such a vast void, he seemed to erase the loneliness. In its place, his words were planted like seeds, watered by the peace in his eyes and nourished by the warmth in his voice.

"Why spend your money on what is not bread and your labor on what does not satisfy? This forsaken place is not your home. We'll make it out of here. I promise."

A bold opening.

I could be bold, too: "I have labored for nothing. Given all my strength in vain. Where is my reward?"

"I hold it in my hands." The fact that they were empty didn't seem to concern him. "You think you will find your escape through victory, but this is not your war to fight. Those who laid waste to you will be far away. Let go. I will fill your open hands."

We walked in silence as I tried to conjure up possible meanings to his words. But he was not finished.

"Let this be written for a future generation, that a people not yet created may praise the Lord."

I have never forgotten.

"As sure as the stars in the sky and the sand on the seashore, I give you the promise of Isaac – out of nothing, I will give you laughter. I will restore your fortunes like streams in the Negev. You have planted tears, but your harvest will be an abundance of joy. Your deserts will become like Eden. The thornbush will be uprooted and a pine tree planted. The briers will die away and myrtle will grow in its place."

In that moment, with all the brokenness inside me, I knew this man offered the restoration and wholeness I craved. I could feel the promises being applied like balm to my wounds. Hope alone was already healing me; I could only imagine the joy that awaited me at the fulfillment of his words.

Yes, I would follow this man wherever he went. He held the words of life.

"Where are you staying tonight?" I asked him.

"Come and you'll see."

Impossible

A promise given
under a star-saturated sky
brightened my eyes with hope,

but a promise delayed
under a thousand dark nights
has dimmed my eyes with despair.

And it's now that you've come
under a cloud-covered moon,
catching my eye with your shaded smile.

Are you Isaac
or just another Ishmael?

T. Jason Vanderlaan

In Which I Think About Your Safety (And Mine)

I've never seen such beauty in spring –
sunlight cutting through the defenses
of my carefully guarded heart.

I am terrified to be your winter,
to pull you back into the shadows,
to hold you just beyond warmth's reach.

I could not bear to wither you
and find that I had withered too.

On the Waters: Ancient and Modern

I.
A flood of sorrow covered my earth
and I stand on the ark of my own solitude,
gazing out over the endless waters,
hoping to catch a glimpse of assurance.

One day, a dove with an olive leaf
will come flying back to me.

II.
I am out of control –
a ship tossed at sea.

Or worse, a sailor onboard,
one weary hand on a wet rail,
slipping towards the hungry waves.

But this is not the end,
not yet, because you are here.

You might be
the hand to help me out,
the hand to hold my heart,
the hand to heal these scars.

This is not the end,
not now, because you are here.

The Aftermath of Graduation

The Virginia countryside blurs by
with my dad on the left,
cows on the right,
and home ahead.

We're putting the miles behind,
reversing the past five years in a single day
and throwing it all away
like sunflower seeds out the window.

James Taylor is on the radio
and I'm lost in a song,
thinking about contracts considered
and promises never made,
wondering if I'll ever figure this out.

My journal lies open –
one page about graduation,
two about a girl on a plane to somewhere
far, far away from me.

I'm measuring the miles between,
recounting the past five days in a single hour
and holding it all inside
like the photo hidden in my wallet.

The song turns to static
and I'm lost in the noise.

Losing What I Never Had

Nothing is left for me here.

The cheers have risen,
the confetti has fallen,
and every reason to stay
just turned around and left
without a word, without a glance,
with a chance to say goodbye.

Gone, slipped away,
like water through the grate,
sand through the fingers,
and love through my heart.

You cannot gather
what cannot be held.

You cannot lose
what you never had.

T. Jason Vanderlaan

Driving North and/or South

I sing
in the sun and the rain
and am equally happy
in both.

I tip my hat to the state line
and keep driving,
eyes straight ahead

except for brief moments
when I glance down
to write poetry
on the back of my hand –

it's worth the risk.

Morning Musings

She would have loved it here,
I know –

the way the morning sun gives life
to steam dancing over hot tea,
while outside the window
two whitetails graze gently, innocently,
in the dew-kissed meadow
just beyond the fence.

I, still in my pajamas,
read poetry from a book,
thick and old and very good.

If she were here,
she'd smile at me
across the kitchen table
and ask me to read one aloud.

But she is not here
and it is for the best.

The day would pass,
the night would come,
and we'd sit on the couch by the fire,
warming the winter from our bones.

I would sit on one side,
she on the other – her hand
always just out of reach.

T. Jason Vanderlaan

Between Lightning and Thunder

For the briefest moment
as lightning flashed across my eyes

I thought I could be
the rainstorm
to make you run
for the shelter
of my arms.

But as the thunder rumbled
in my weathered bones,
the sun broke through
my clouded mind:

I am simply
a single drop,
falling foolishly
from a darkened sky
to kiss your cheek

and be wiped away,
forgotten.

My Blood is Yellow; Hers is Hidden

Give me a moment
and I'll analyze it to death,
slice it into pieces until the parts
no longer represent the whole.

You travel above the clouds,
and I am invariably left
to wonder what comes next.

I have no bags to pack,
no ticket to clutch tight,
no destination to distract,
only a stationary heart.

Waiting is the hardest start,
and beginnings are always fragile
even without silent preludes.

I want to believe that you're still there
across the unspoken,
but flight patterns have shown
that those who leave
never come back to me.

All I have is this great distance –
unable to see far enough
to catch a glimpse of your smile
or the lack thereof.

T. Jason Vanderlaan

Are Those the Stars I See Reflected in Your Eyes or Just the City Lights?

I've been mistaken
once, twice, third time's a charm
and I am charmed

by the sparkle in your eyes
that makes me wonder
if I should hold my doubts in doubt
and believe everything you've left unsaid.

Or maybe you're the one misled
by my paper heart, ink blood –
distractions to keep you at a distance
from skin, warm but flawed.

I remember thinking I could keep you safe
written in a poem, folded up, stored in a box.

Maybe you could do the same:
hide me away in words,

but when you return, unfold,
I think you'll discover I've faded
much faster than the ink.

Feather(wait)

In this silence you are
featherweight.

I hold my breath,

afraid even the slightest word
could tip the balance
and send you away from me.

T. Jason Vanderlaan

Misplaced Metaphors

Out on the lake in a borrowed boat,
I row. You watch me,
I watch the sky – cloudy, only
a few stars peeking through.

You hint at possibilities
and imply another attempt,
not knowing how vulnerable I am tonight.
But I would know then as now
we only make the best mistakes.

My oars sink in deep, propelling us
across dark waters
to a destination unknown;
we should turn back
and tie up at the shore,
but momentum pushes for more.

I look to the sky again,
no change, but I think I see
why this moment feels
so out of place:

you're not Isaac
but you're not Ishmael, either.

And that's the hardest part.

Her Smile was Like a Letter Written in a Foreign Language

I don't know when
you're coming back,
or if you'll dock your boat
on my shore again.

Winds blow
and storms can change
your mind, your heart,
your course back to me.

There is nothing
I can do, but
watch you go
and wonder at the way
I feel like this has happened before.

Of Descent or Promise

I am filled with unfulfilled words,
dormant, though not forever –
their light shines upon another day.

Though it lingers, I will wait.
It will certainly come.

III.

The Soil From Which I've Grown

Nuclear Bombs and Nuclear Families

My own personal Nagasaki,
a Hiroshima hit to the center
of my seven-year-old universe.

Instant devastation
as the mushroom cloud rose
like a headstone over our home.

Then, the fallout –
years of residual radiation,
poisoning me with decay.

There is no escape from the ashes
of a family set on fire.

I will always be haunted
by memories like shadows
burned into stone:

the accumulating sorrow and guilt of
my father,
my mother,
my sister,
my heart soaking it all in.

You cannot run from the heat,
from the hurt, from the hollow
ache inside, constantly repeating:

There is no escape.

T. Jason Vanderlaan

Restless

Always on the move, always temporary –
roots sent down, pulled back up.

Home is fluid, the inherent instability learned
from the back and forth of a custody childhood.

It isn't that I want to keep leaving, but
I find comfort in wandering, in its familiarity,
in knowing it is safer than being uprooted.

Developing Old Photographs

Slowly fading into view, revealing
a past more black than gray.
Each image tells a story,
each brings to view memories
forgotten or never known:

Courthouses, judges, lawyers
stealing my childhood,
realizing mine is not the only one lost –
weathered, a butterfly's wings in motion;
years later, the wind rips the breath from my lungs.

Grown-up eyes looking at me,
knowing more than they told.
They held secrets I could not bear,
though I think I bore them still.

The Mathematics of Divorce

I have a hard time listening to people talk about the devastating mathematics of divorce. Like it is just another subject to learn about in school. Reading and writing are learned in a classroom, but I learned arithmetic at home.

It started with division. And fractions, as I watched my family splinter and separate. The two who were one became two again. The children were the remainders – they always are in division.

Family became: Mom in one place, Dad in another; then the ever mobile, ever movable, always transportable sister and me. Home became Homes. Birthday became Birthdays, and Christmas became Christmases.

My sister and I didn't complain. After all, two are better than one (at least that's what we told anyone who asked), but what I wouldn't have given just to have one Christmas, one Birthday, one Home again. Sometimes more is less, and addition can be subtraction.

I was soon to learn more of subtraction. The unshakable feeling that we – that I – was now incomplete, somehow less than before. Always removable, detracted. Forever diminishing. Never whole again.

I learned addition by counting the tears of those I loved and could not heal. Though I did not cry, I learned to multiply the pain inside. To pile sorrow upon sorrow, compound interest. A big gain on the return.

I soon grew proficient at algebra, too, as I learned to balance the equation, to calculate the days spent with each parent, to ensure they were the same on both sides, being careful to account for any variables such as times of arrival and departure, as well as perceptions of quality over quantity.

So you can talk about the statistics all you want. Half of first marriages. Two-thirds of second ones. Three-fourths of the not-so-charmed third tries. The children of divorced parents: double the chance.

Those numbers are only shadows to me. I live the reality. I've got the mathematics in my blood. I've got the statistics pumping through my veins. No matter how many times I bleed, I can never get them out.

T. Jason Vanderlaan

The Planting of Weeds

Silent, watching
everything fall apart,
powerless to hold up
even a single crumbling wall,

I learn the meaning of my name,
and what it means to be unable to heal,
what it means to not be enough.

I learn that love
can fall, can break.

I learn to be afraid, to strive,
to arrange and control –
if love has conditions,
maybe I can prove my worth,
maybe I can earn the right to stay.

Chain Gang Dirge

The crimes of my father
and his father and his father
and his father – they are in me now,
chains in my veins,
stains within my stains.

I have become
just another link in the line
carrying out my sentence
as we march to the music
of who we were
and who we are
and who we will be.

T. Jason Vanderlaan

Two Decades Later

There is no tenure, no immunity
when it comes to divorce
and its inescapable wake.

I still count days
to balance the equation,
but it cannot be.

For to give is to take
and the loss is always felt.

Love Again

Despite all the broken limbs
scattered beneath this family tree,
there is love in what remains,
and there is love in grafted branches.

Together we grow, reach
out and up, intertwined,
tangled and beautiful,
strengthened by each choice
to love and love again.

A Father's Gifts

I.
Eighty-five percent of men in prison
grew up without a father.

This was never an option in your mind.

You drove hours to see my sister and me:
bowtie donuts, school plays, baseball games.

Hours to spend moments with us.
Hours for us.

Your love was in the miles,
in the minutes we cherished together.

II.
Graduating with a Theology degree,
my present from you:
not a commentary set or a new suit.

Instead:
a lever-action .44 rifle.

Perfect.

III.
All day together on Smokey's Run Farm,
chainsaws in hand, fallen trees at our feet:

Good, hard work.

As the evening descended, you told me:
I'd work with you in the woods any day.

Beth-Anne

I.
Two-years old, I ask,
Can I hold it?
not knowing I'd been given
much more than a sister.

A constant companion,
the only part of home that never changed;
no matter where I was, she
was always at my side.

II.
My sister: full of grace –
beautiful, brave, and captivating

with the elegance of a dancer,
enraptured in the joy of her Savior,

and the fiery courage of a lover
whose heart is consecrated to God.

Your pure and passionate faith
inspires me in the depths of my soul.

I am blessed to call you sister,
I am blessed to call you friend.

Pappa Bear

We share no blood
but you love me
like I was yours from birth.

I have watched you standing guard
over the hearts of this family –

you cherish my mother,
you love all your children,
you offer your strength to protect.

In my eyes and in my heart,
you will always be my Pappa Bear:
strong, wise, and godly.

We share no blood
but I love you
like I was yours from birth.

Mama (You Carried Me)

You carried me for nine months,
but I was in your heart
long before I was in your arms.

You loved me
before I was born,
like Hannah praying for a son.

God gave me to you,
and gave you to me,
like Moses had his mother.

You carried me for nine months,
but that was just the beginning –
you taught me with your words, your life,
your unceasing love for a growing boy.

You led me with your scars,
like a pillar of fire,
as I gained wounds of my own.

You led me with your tears,
like a cloud of comfort,
as I shed sorrows of my own.

You showed me
that we could leave these deserts behind.

You carried me for nine months.
You carry me still.

T. Jason Vanderlaan

A Man Shall Leave

These roots go far below the surface,
anchoring in the soil from which I've grown,
in the soil that is my foundation, the source
of wounds and weaknesses,
of healing and strength.

But now I grow
restless. And ready.

This will always be home,
but I was made to leave,
to find other soil to join,
to put my roots down
to plant my own home.

IV.

Now You Can Pretend
Like You Knew Me All Along

Concrete Boy

The day and the years coincide
but this is not a prophecy or prediction.
This is simply me, sitting, staring
at the gap between
the dominoes that have fallen
and the ones still standing.

T. Jason Vanderlaan

I Feel the Weight of Every Word, Double-Edged

Listen to every word
of my unspoken confessions
and you will hear, not triumph,
but the deepest of regret.

Read between the lines
and you'll see secrets darker
than I could bear to unveil.

The Wanderer: Hunger

He told me, "I wander because you wander. I was born to be like you. To be with you."

Sometimes I take comfort in his presence. Sometimes I am angry. I wish he'd disappear behind the curtain and pull a few strings – to lift this veil, or tighten this noose. Anything but this endless unknown, this gnawing hunger for something more. I know he has the power to give me more than this.

But he doesn't. He just keeps walking, only a few steps ahead, repeating all his unfulfilled words.

Now I notice others, whispering from the shadows, beckoning me away from his side. They speak of stones turned to bread.

I slow my pace. Let the distance grow.

T. Jason Vanderlaan

When I Look Into the Eyes That Cannot See Me

In this digital approximation of intimacy,
I find, for a moment, fulfillment –
manufactured and synthetic, an imitation
enough to steal my eyes away.

Then the image is gone,
the illusion vanishes,
and I am hollow again.

She offers me everything,
gives me all but what I need.

Every time I look,
I feed a hunger I cannot fill.

She is Power Over Me

Sitting on the edge of the bed,
head in hands,
I stare down at the unlaced shoes
I never should have taken off.

Never should have let this night unfold,
lure us in, enshrouding every glance
in promises we say but never mean.

She is asleep now,
but she does not dream of me.
Whatever she says, I know
she despises me, that I am
as empty to her as she is to me.

I slip out of the window,
close it behind me.

But I will be back,
and we will keep pretending
to find pleasure in our ruin.

T. Jason Vanderlaan

The Grass Isn't Greener,
It's Just a Different Shade of Dead

I.
I take a bow
as the Pharisees nod and smile,
because I can shed my skin,
but the skeleton stays the same.

II.
I, Victim.

But I am giver and receiver of scars.
I know what it feels like to hold the knife –
the handle just as sharp as the blade.

I, Villain.

III.
A rat in the shadows, at home
in the filth of the streets.

I can make you see me
and leave me at the curb
as drizzle becomes downpour
and I slip into the city drains.

IV.
There is no penance,
though I give what remains,
though I dedicate the rest of my life,
there is no restitution
for these crimes.

Whoever you are,
listen, but do not follow.

Cast the First Stone

I don't know if I can take
another approving nod,
another admiring smile.

You stand there acquitting me,
but you don't know the half of it:
I hide more hell inside than you imagine.

I wrote my sins in black, bound them in a book.
Do you need it written in the sand?

Or do you finally realize
I claim the worst of these confessions,
I still own the darkest of my stories?

Take the condemnation clenched in your hands
and turn from this woman in the dirt,
this woman dragged from my bed.

Let the stones be cast upon my head.

T. Jason Vanderlaan

You Told Me You Loved Me

I think, perhaps,
what bothers me most
is not that you proved false,
but that I became false for you.

I woke to shadows coming for me
and as I was taken, I saw you standing there:
razor in hand, my hair at your feet,
your face contorted
somewhere between relief and regret.

It was the last face I ever saw.

6 Reasons Why You Shouldn't Date a Poet

1. **Poetry**. As much as you may enjoy poetry, you must realize it is a farce created by poets to lure you into a deadly trap. The gift itself is the poison, and a relationship built upon such duplicity is bound for destruction. Consider this fair warning: whatever you are expecting, you will be disappointed. And I quote, "Getting to know you is like travelling through space, and just when I think I've reached a safe planet to land on, I discover a black hole instead."

2. **Family Dinners**. Poets are not the kind of guys you want to take home to meet your parents. They live almost entirely in their minds, engrossed in emotional symbols and metaphors. Thus, they don't have a lot to add to dinner table discussions about the real world. Sure, it can be deceptively fascinating to read poetry, but there is no doubt it makes poor conversation. In fact, poets write so excessively in hopes that they won't be asked to speak at all. If they do have to speak, however, it takes twice as long to formulate thoughts that aren't even half as coherent as their written ones.

3. **Financial Stability**. Being a poet is hardly a legitimate career choice and it certainly won't instill great confidence in parents wishing to ensure their daughter's

future security and well-being. And I quote, "Jason* has a real job now? Huh, well I'm surprised. I didn't think he was ever going to do anything in life." It isn't called the starving artist routine for nothing. But this is not a condition we should pity; poets will often neglect or even turn down stable sources of income just so they can dedicate time to writing a book that will never produce an income anyway.

4. **Reliability**. Really, poets don't offer stability of any kind. They thrive on melancholic endorphins. They enjoy even their sadness. While they admit that this is pretty twisted, they insist they like it that way. Poets are dissatisfied with the status-quo, which means they are continually seeking discontentment; happiness may be their dream but when it approaches, they find a way to escape. And I quote, "Self-sabotage is totally your personality disorder." Is that really the kind of life you want to join?

5. **Passive-Aggressiveness**. Poets express their unvoiced feelings through poetry, most of which the recipient will never see. Even the words that are seen are cloaked in so much obscurity as to make them indiscernible. Nonetheless, the poet will live as if the recipient had seen and understood all, and resent the fact that nothing has changed. Then the poet will write even

more poetry, thus perpetuating both his passion and this destructive cycle.

6. **Self-Obsession**. Sure, everyone has baggage, but poets immortalize it in ink and enshrine it upon paper thrones. When the music plays, you must bend the knee. Poets are egotistically focused on themselves. Besides compiling their random thoughts into books and expecting people to pay hard-earned cash for the "privilege" of reading them, they generally orient their entire daily lives around self-promotion. Poets try to be self-abasing in an attempt to appear humble, but in actuality they know that self-deprecation and self-aggrandizement are really twins. They are very good at using clever disguises, though, to conceal their self-centeredness. For example, a poet might make a list entitled "6 Reasons Why You Shouldn't Date a Poet" when what he really means is "6 Reasons Why You Shouldn't Date Me."

*Names have *not* been changed in order to incriminate the guilty. Call it "poetic justice" if you will, since poets do not respect others' privacy. If you get too close to a poet, your life (both the good and the bad) *will* end up in poetry for all to read. This is as inevitable as it is despicable.

Intoxibilities

I.
Intoxication: possibilities.

I am under no delusion
that I would leave behind
even a single broken heart
if I walked away.

Though I do wonder
what might happen
if I stayed.

II.
A jump-start desire –
no follow through,
though I can lay out each step.

What matters though
is not her laugh
(or even her)
but that I spoke
what was in my head.

Intoxication. New frontier.
New self.

III.
New confusion.

Because all the while
I feel like a betrayer,
unfaithful
for every sip: sweet.

The path splits, splinters
and I'm still looking
for one –
which one?

Have I become the culprit
for enjoying this moment?

Intoxication.

T. Jason Vanderlaan

Un(limit)ed

In the morning
we are all less grand
with our suits and dresses
back in the closet
or crumpled on the floor.

Already the faces fade,
dissipating with the emotional charge
of such a fine evening.

We pack our bags, relishing
and regretting what could have been.

Perhaps the magic is in the distance,
in the unlimited possibility:
enticing as long as it remains
untested, just beyond our grasp.

Implementing Emergency Exit Plans

Chalk it up
to another caution-tape parade,
to the celebration of warning signs
and the praise of trespassing notices.

Perhaps the safest course
would have been to tell you
I'm a model citizen.

In the silence, the sirens sing,
announcing pending departures.

I put my ear to the wall
and carve another mark in the row,
add another line to my sentence,
cut another notch in the belt
of a man living out another's name.

Every breath, an attempt.
Every endeavor, a prison.

Even in my sleep
the years play out before my eyes
like forgeries, like chalk lines.

Caution: Entreaty

You have me
backed into a corner, listening to
your sweet tones and best intentions.

But it is I who have lured you here
with every one of my insecurities,
so enticing – a wounded animal
cannot be ignored, or trusted.

You may know my name,
but that doesn't mean you can heal me.

Would you stay even if you couldn't?

Magnet Poetry on the Carpet

I: a young boy.
She: a porcelain fever.

Two prisoners,
broken animals.

I lie
to the ghost of morning,
linger in dirt and salt.

I would ask
to wake.

New Every Morning

The handle and the blade take on new meaning
as I wipe the mirror and raise the razor
to meet the face staring back at me.

Life flows, halts
in patterns –

Down, across,
right to left.
Down, across,
left to right.

Clean the upper lip.
Down, down, down,
always down.

Slow under,
hesitate at the throat,
finish the job.

Rinse it all down the drain.
Just like that.

A fresh start
with only a few new cuts.

Shadows and Scars

These are the shadows
that saturate:

I reached for the hand,
outstretched,
and followed it down,
deep into this darkness.

One day,
when I'm gone,
I'll sing of these shadows
as things of the past,
distant and dead.

And these are the scars
that separate:

I reached for the hand,
withdrawn,
and found myself alone,
stranded in this darkness.

One day,
when they're gone,
I'll sing of these scars,
as a thing of the past,
far and forgotten.

T. Jason Vanderlaan

If I Were a Famous Musician,
This Would Be My Application to the Club

IIIx
Sinope concluded that the absence of passion
was better than incomplete passion
and I tend to agree,
though I've been known to digress.

But I can never wander far
from the truths and the riddles:

When every bone in your grip is broken,
your weeping will be quenched.
When you are out of outs,
you will find your way in.

IIIx
Twenty seven new books
and twenty seven old letters
stuffed into an envelope
with a Claude Pepper stamp:
a warning – a blessing – from
the lips of Abbé Faria, eleven
years too early, never too late.

III.
I take a stand, open
to amendments, fundamentally
opposed to closing my eyes
or staring straight ahead.

All around, dead ends
and endless possibilities.

Hide and Seek

I win.

And by winning,
I lose.

Because I wanted
to be found.

T. Jason Vanderlaan

Unread

I promised myself
it would never happen this way again,
but there you are
with ink on your fingertips,
and all my skin is still my own.

To know and be known –
ever alluring, ever elusive.

You leaf through the pages,
but my eyes are still unread.

V.

Detours & Detox

Should You Have the Right
to Let Me Break Your Heart?

I think you like me
because I'm broken.

I think you want me
because I hide.

I am keeping you at arm's length –
not because I don't want to let you in,
but because I am too afraid
of the backdoor out.

You always leave
my head spinning.

You see through
my inky walls
as if they were transparent.

You draw me
out of the shadows.

Sometimes, when I'm dizzy,
I want to tell you everything.

T. Jason Vanderlaan

September Stars

The city shoreline is lit up for us tonight,
if that's the kind of thing you like,
and the smell of anticipation is in the air,
though I think we both caught a different scent.

You call me by name.

Just imagine, everything in perfect place –
each grain of sand moves with precision
beneath our carefree footsteps,

Each crashing wave echoes across the night
as the moon aligns with our shadows
and the sky expands above our heads.

You say my name.

This could be ours for the taking
but I am already taken
by the stars above my head,
however dim they may be.

I'll buy you a drink tonight
but in the morning this will just be a memory
fading into the ever retreating past.

You may know my name,
but that doesn't mean
I can heal you.

In Which I Can't Decide Which Metaphor to Use, So I Use Both and Find that Neither Satisfies

I.
I've been face to face
with this brick wall for
daysmonthsyears, growing
weary, dizzy staring at the pattern
of defeat, dead ends.

Now the wall is tumbling,
each brick falling, forming paths
away from this place.

Endless options, but
now I'm not sure I want to leave.

II.
Immobilized by mobilization,
I find that more of my roots have taken hold
than I could have ever foreseen.

Still I rise, despite the tearing
tendrils, despite the protest
of bark twisting, cracking, snapping.

I pull and the earth pulls back.

T. Jason Vanderlaan

Alone Together

The smell of burning theories,
the distinct odor of acceleration
incinerating ideals.

You can hear the sound,
the squeal, the wail
as if to mourn the passing,
the rush that never moves
until it leaves us both
standing alone together
in the rearview mirror.

Truthful Disguises

Honesty is the lie we tell each other
to maintain the illusion
that we have nothing left to hide.

You always saw the best in me,
always believed the worst.
Your affection, your disdain –
all aimed at an imaginary me.

I've folded myself in layers
thick enough to disguise,
tight enough to conceal.

But you can unravel me,
stretch me out across the sky,
thin enough to see through
all I've kept from you.

T. Jason Vanderlaan

The Constellation of All My Misplaced Hopes

I.
Each of you shining in your own right, but
together: a pattern of fate
and all the choices we've made.

II.
Another tall tower,
soft voice in a dark window,
but long hair let down
is no promise of an invitation
once you reach the top.

III.
Arms crossed in a metaphor,
disappointment in your eyes,
like tears about to spill

You look away.
I understand.

I will not be your Ishmael.

IV.
I'm your sure bet,
your safety net.

V.
Caught between
the girl I can save
and the girl who can save me.

VI.
Each of you
lining up.

Each of you
taking flight to somewhere
far away from me.

VII.
I'm falling for you
like a shooting star.

So make a wish
before I burn out.

Close your eyes
but when you look again,
I'll be gone.

T. Jason Vanderlaan

While I Remain Silent, Like a Friend or Enemy

And so he misinterprets, thinking
she wants him to take her advice,
when she really wants him to take her.

You and I are not so different.

Full of knowledge and words and desires;
unable to drink from the empty glasses
we keep lifting to our lips.

Yet neither of us leaves. We keep
forgetting to remember
things we've always known:
the only ones worth waiting for
are those willing to wait.

For the First Time Again

Upstairs, I have retreated
from your arrival. Blindly,
I saw you, and saw the scales
fall from my eyes.

I need a moment to breathe,
to purge the poison from my veins,
ashamed of how easily I wander.

You make me want to be good again.
You make me believe that I could.

Around the corner,
I hesitate and listen to your voice,
clear and light, piercing through
the walls of my mistakes.

My eyes are open
for the first time again.

All I see is you.

T. Jason Vanderlaan

She

She moves like the wind
and I am the empty arms
of a winter tree, lacking
even leaves for her to rustle
as she passes through.

Unraveling

The darkness swells behind me,
calling me back,
calling me away from the light
that has so gracefully – perhaps
so unintentionally – fallen across my face.

Only now do I realize
how thin a thread
has been holding me to you.

T. Jason Vanderlaan

On the Benefits and Heartache of Being a Pyro

Floating
in a room full of people
as far as they are close,
I am a stranger despite commonalities.

Settling,
I take comfort in the familiar,
in being asked to start a fire,
in watching flames embrace logs,
in the promise of heat and smoke.

Rising,
I wish to be carried away,
to be held, enveloped,
to be consumed so entirely.

The Wanderer: Not Without Keen Suffering

"Is it right for you to be angry?" The morning sun silhouetted him against the cloudless sky.

"Of course it is. I've spent years looking for shelter, for reprieve from this desert heat. Finally, I've found shade beneath these leaves, only to have them wither overnight."

"I know what you want, but there is no peace for you in this place."

"But I am responsible for–"

"There is nothing more you can do here. I have heard you and I will bless all you leave behind, but you must let go."

Leaving has never been so hard.

Many nights later, sitting by the fire, I begin to feel a sense of something like closure. Like I could watch the embers fade and find peace in the darkness, in having nothing left, in knowing that the night is as dark as a blank slate.

For Closure

You used to write me poetry – invitations
into your vulnerability. I thought:
maybe I can be strong again.

You assembled me with grace, as if
you understood even all the missing pieces.
Thrilling to think you might.

But I could not pay what I promised
and I watched you go,
willing and unwilling.

I want you to know: I see you
and I know that God's gaze
has been upon your face
and He is well pleased.

And I, even if only for a moment,
am thankful to have rested
in the shade of your blossoming.

So don't worry, dear Lucie,
this is not complicated for me:
you are beautiful
when you are happy.

I hope you find your way
away from me.

Wish: Love

There you wait with wings to be unfurled.
I see in you potential as boundless as the sky
and I wish for you all of it.

Love is not a cage.
It does not make you less,
does not require clipped wings.

Love is the open air, the wind.
It always expands, lifts you up,
gives you the space to become more.
Love smiles at your newfound strength,
cheers your newly attained heights.

Love knows the difference between being
the branch that keeps you tethered
and the branch that launches you into flight.

T. Jason Vanderlaan

Autumn Rain Falling

I.
You are a mystery to me, perhaps
only because I am a dreamer.

You send me words, saturated with potential,
and return my words, read but not cherished.

Only an hour earlier, you confessed
and let me pretend in the dark
to be brave enough for us both.

Maybe I was.

Only an hour later, you speak
with just enough conviction
to persuade my foolish heart.

Give me a reason to stay.

II.
Disenchanted and it's okay.
though I still waver,
because I see buds upon the leaves.

I wonder what it would have meant to stay.

But my hands are tied
to the steering wheel
as I drive away, always
on the move, always away.

I am glad to have planted these trees,
even if I never share their shade with you.

Let His Words Drain into the Gutter
(Drink Every Drop, but Leave the Cup on the Table)

She stirs her coffee, slowly,
like a metaphor I can't quite understand,
while I watch the steam rise and fade
in the morning sunlight, disappearing
like last night's rain.

Tucking her hair behind her ear – even
her clichés are beautiful – she lifts
the cup to her lips, invites the moment in.

Her eyes are soft and brave,
but they are strangers to her smile,
as if she'd cast her pearls
at one too many less-than-great men.

I want to tell her:
Don't sell yourself short.
You deserve to be happy.
You deserve the best.

And while I am arrogant enough
to think of walking over
and paying the bill, as if
I could cancel all her debts
(maybe even a few of my own),

I don't believe
my words can be offered
from anywhere but this distance –
close enough to convey,
far enough to retain their meaning.

VI.

Goodbyes, Farewells,
and Other Beginnings

A Boy Who No Longer Exists, Writing to a Girl Who Never Did

Lying next to me,
you make half-conscious promises
not to take me for granted this time.

You whisper, *I love you.*
I respond by reflex,
but my heart is gone.

While you sleep,
I cut the rope that keeps me tethered
between you on the cliff above
and the great unknown below.

Except, I do know
what waits below: my death
and everything after that.

Digression

She told me
flowers mourned their death,
robbed from the earth,
sacrificed on the unworthy altar of romance.

I wondered
if they found honor in death,
longing their whole lives
for a chance to make that sacrifice.

My Exodus

Fire and ice have fallen
but you're still lukewarm,
with your Pharaoh heart
and your Israelite skin.

So do what you will
but I cannot stay any longer.

This is my exodus
from your barren lands.

Darkness and light reveal
but you're still blind,
with your Pharaoh eyes
and your Israelite smile.

So be what you will
but I will not stay any longer.

This is my exodus
from you.

T. Jason Vanderlaan

The End of a Matter is Better Than Its Beginning

I.
Release my lungs
and let me scream
these songs of closure.

II.
I have dulled my sword
on your stone tower,

and all my cries
for you to come down
have fallen upon defeated ears.

III.
If you get burned enough times
you'll eventually learn
to release the coal
that refuses to cool.

IV.
I must admit,
as I bid you farewell,
it's never felt so good
to feel nothing
as it does right now.

V.
Call it what you want,
but I will call it release –
sweet, beautiful release.

Like Ashes to the Wind

I have lived for far too long
in overestimation of your underestimation.

You are not my final verdict.

These memories will burn
on the altar of promises,
and the flames will be hot enough
to dry my tears.

Dreams burn bright
when they're dying away,
and like ashes to the wind,
I will learn to hope anew.

T. Jason Vanderlaan

Magnet Poetry on the Wall

May a bitter woman's winter rose
never tempt your love away.

The petals in her frantic storm
smell of death and decay
and she will smooth and deceive
your spring dreams away.

Her deceptive beauty is nothing but death.

So farewell, my iron beauty,
haste away, my discontented lover.

(Un)Casting Pearls

If I could have just one wish tonight,
I would plead for a chance to go back,
pick these pearls out of the mud,
clean them off, and return them
to the cavity of my heart.

Maybe then
it wouldn't hurt so much
to walk away.

A Cloak to Disguise

For too long I blamed you
for making me feel like I had to be
someone else for you.

I always had the choice to be myself,
just as you had the right
to choose what you wanted.

For years, I tried to prove
you were wrong.

I thought I was trying
to convince you; really
it was I who doubted.

I wore my anger at you
as a cloak to disguise
my disappointment in myself.

Further Proof

What naïve arrogance
to think I could contain
all my regret in a single glass.

Every girl I've ever cared about
stands before me in a haze of guilt.

I have failed
even in attempts to protect –
just another way to wound,
to give them scars to match my own.

Terrifying to think of those
I have pushed away
or kept at a distance.

Too afraid to be the stain
beneath another hand clutched to chest,
too afraid to be that close to pain
dealt from my own hands.

I thought about their safety
and acted on my own.

I carry this weight inside –
heavier, more terrible
than any of them will ever know.

I am drunk with regret.

T. Jason Vanderlaan

The Bridge Between Us
(To the tune of Samuel Barber's *Adagio for Strings, Op. 11*)

Flames rise to meet falling rain
like two long-lost lovers,
like an incomplete reunion,
each reaching out, grasping,
yearning to embrace all that is missing
inside their own souls.

The crackling of burning wood and rope,
the pitter-patter of the rain, both
speaking their own language,
hoping to be understood, to be known,
knowing they are forever separated
by the passion that first attracted.

But for the night, for the moment
they dance together in that place
between the dirt and the clouds,
where the sky kisses the earth.

The lightning tears through the heavens,
thunder cracks and booms – a warning,
a threat – and the flames respond with
their own popping and snapping, defiant
in spite of – perhaps because of –
comparative insignificance.

I close my eyes, and my skin is fire,
the downpour only drenching the surface,
never penetrating, never permeating,
yet persistent, desperate to get in, while I,
by my very nature, forbid entrance.

I burn, tremulous inferno, so blistering
even you cannot soothe my ache,
though you continue to fall, merciful
and gracious, tender even in your strength.

I burn deeper.
I cannot leave anything behind.

I open my eyes , look through the flames.
You are still on the other side, the sky
soaking your hair and face, tears
falling like promises, like forgiveness.

If I could reach you, I'd wipe them all away.

T. Jason Vanderlaan

Sickness Unto Death

Six feet under the dirt of my regrets,
I buried my second chance ages ago.
I've spent the years since
filling the graveyard with her siblings.

Now I return again,
holding in my hands such perfect plans.
All worthless now.

Incurable Wounds

His frown is not unkind,
but it crushes me nonetheless.

He breaks the words
tumbling from my lips,
and I am grateful.

The night of His eyes
falls over every broken piece.

In His shadow, I am lost and found.

When He speaks,
His voice is like the sunrise
upon my blinded eyes.

In His words, I am slain and raised to life:

Both given and received,
these wounds are incurable,
but there is healing in My hands
for every scar.

T. Jason Vanderlaan

A Brief Glimpse Backwards As We Move Forward

Don't let this be our last goodbye.

I want to see you on the other side,
when time is a distant memory
and we've gathered around a table
to celebrate all things new.

But before the first toast is made,
we'll glance back on all we've done
and weep at the cost.

Our tears will be many,
but He will wipe away each one.

The Opportunity to Defeat Your Enemy

If you are thrown in a pit,
sold into slavery,
falsely accused,
and locked up in prison,

it is my prayer
that you will come face to face
with those who have wronged you,

and that you will have
the strength and the grace
to forgive them.

Stumbling Towards Forgiveness

Resentment is a poison to drink,
but forgiving you feels like a toxin of its own.

I want you out.

Let me rest in peace,
away from your embrace,
away from your cold shoulder.

I was never your enemy and I never will be,
but that doesn't mean I trust you.

I was so addicted to your inconsistency –
you taught me to believe in love and apathy.

I'm still so addicted to the flaws you saw in me.

Some say, *Forgive and forget*,
but maybe forgiveness is to remember –
to acknowledge, to burn, to ache,
to embrace the sorrow,

and then let go.

A Better Now

Forgiveness is not to be unwounded,
but to live with a scar.

It is less like cleaning out the attic,
more like reframing an old painting,
moving it to a different room in the house.

Less like arriving at the mountaintop,
more like the decision to climb
and every step that follows.

I am tired of insisting you stay in the past;
finally, I am ready to release you
to be as real as all the good and bad
I see in myself.

I insist,
not on a better past,
but on a better now.

I will not demand repayment or remedy
as prerequisite – to forgive a debt
is to cancel it unpaid.

Here's the truth: I've committed
crimes far worse than yours.

This doesn't excuse
the wrong you've done,

but it does mean
neither of us deserves
the grace we've been given.

T. Jason Vanderlaan

For Years, by Inches. Then in Hours, Miles.

Let's pause for a moment,
pretend we never lost our innocence,
pretend we never put up our guard,
never took for granted,
never thought too much of ourselves.

Let's sit here for a moment.

Let the truth sink in
when we can no longer pretend.

Please forgive me;
I forgive you.

VII.

Shelter

I Used to Believe Love Could Never Die

I find her in a rundown old house –
cracked windows, chipped paint,
door ajar, creaking floorboards
announcing my entrance.

Across the room, she welcomes me
with a smile as crippled as her movement.
She shuffles with a cane – slow, painfully slow.

I move towards her, but too late.
She stumbles, topples to the floor,
lays there motionless, broken, resigned.

I fear she will never rise again.

The Wanderer: Question

The desert wind was growing cold, like falling out of love. The small fire cast more light than heat, yet even as he stirred the coals in a continuous cycle of life and death, no light pierced the charcoal shadows cast over our faces.

"What are you looking for?" he asked.

It had been a long day. I wasn't interested in his games tonight. Not interested in his questions about things that he and I already knew the answers to.

"I've told you a hundred times."

"No, I mean: what are you looking for in *me*?"

New in New: Intoxicated Rambling in the Wake of a Beautiful Rumor

Slouched in the corner, sipping
old wine from an
old wineskin, hidden in an
old brown bag, clutched in my
old Pharisee hands,

I must conclude: the
old is better.

Better than pouring new wine into
old wineskins
and watching it break the skin,
run down my hands and arms
like blood,
like inevitable regret.

Better than staring down
at my inability to hold, to keep,
to know what it's like
to finally be known.

Better than longing for a taste
that never stays long enough
to find my lips.

Better at easing the pain
of wanting something better.

Horizon Watch

Waiting
in silence and shadow.

Always waiting
for You to show up,
to come through,
to come over the horizon,
pulling the dawn behind You
like a majestic cape.

Waiting to see
if You'll come at all.

To Only Want One Thing

Gasoline and a match,
starting over from scratch –
beautiful as it rushes in to greet me,
to defeat me, to give me
the only thing I've ever wanted.

The Wanderer: Desperation

I shove him hard and he falls on his back. He does not resist my anger.

"You led me into this!" I shout. "And maybe I ruined my chances, or maybe there was never a chance to start with, but it doesn't matter. If you knew the seed would not grow, why did you let me plant it? Why did you water it if you were just going to tear it from the ground as soon as it sprouted?"

Standing over him, I feel justified. He does not rise, but replies in calm tones. "You have planted much, but harvest little. You eat, but are unfulfilled. You drink and still thirst. You put on clothes and remain cold. You gather treasures, only to put them in a bag full of holes."

He hasn't answered my accusations at all. I'm not sure if I'm more or less angry, though. His words reveal my grief so accurately that I feel weak under their weight. I sink to my knees next to him.

"I am so tired of making memories I can't keep."

He waits for me to realize the deeper truth.

"I am so tired of this void that can never be filled."

"All this time, you've been searching for validation, for somewhere to belong, for someone to know you and love you enough to stay. But all along I've been here by your side."

"Yeah, of course. I know you love me," I say dismissively. "You've wandered with me all these years. But I still have this emptiness."

He looks at me as if I'm still avoiding His implied question.

"Yes, yes. I *know* you love me."

Still, he sits silent, waiting.

More slowly, quietly now, I say in a cracking voice: "I know you love me." I avert my eyes as they fill with tears. "It's just that… I don't know. I've really needed you, and you haven't shown up. But I understand, I guess. After all I've done, how could you still want me?"

"Oh, my child…" He stretches out his arms, his hands. I see the scars.

"That's just the thing!" I cry. "I did that to you!"

"You may have done it to me, but that doesn't mean I didn't also choose it. I chose this," he says, looking at his hands, then back at me, "because I wanted to be with you. Because I love you. That will never change."

I have no more words left. Only tears.

He wraps me in his arms.

It feels like coming clean, like coming up for air. It feels like coming home.

Walking Away

The light is so soft
I can hardly bear its gentle touch
upon my face, warmth
ever so inviting.

Despite the chill
at my back, here between
what has been and what could be,
I don't turn away.

In this beauty,
I could lose myself.
I could find myself.
I could belong.
I could–

He places His hand on my shoulder,
turns to me with a smile of sadness and myrrh:
Come, we have work to do.

I try to read His face: indiscernible,
a mystery always hidden in His eyes.

I nod, but still I remain, turning back
to gaze upon the world just beyond my grasp,
letting the moments slip away uncounted.

His hand squeezes my shoulder firmly,
meaning: *If I lead you away, I can lead you back,*
or just as easily: *Take your last look, son of Moses.*

We turn – warmth retreating
from my face – and return to darkness.

I want to ask a hundred questions, but
His eyes are already set ahead, and I know
those questions hold no answers yet.

Sukkot

Weary under the desert sun,
I have searched for comfort
beneath a thousand shelters,
both true and false – none
enough to give me rest.

Only in You.

Tent and wings, shield and shade,
I find shelter in Your words.
I find shelter in You.

Good Soil

All my attempts:
devoured,
withered,
choked.

All dead ends
find life in You.

Plant me in Your heart
and plant Your heart in me.

T. Jason Vanderlaan

The Gifts of the Promised Land

I will taste the harvest of promise
in this land or the next,
but there are some first fruits
even sweeter than milk and honey.

To walk towards the gift
with the Giver by your side
is to already have everything.

He fills the void that every desire tries to fill,
and any emptiness exists
only because He has opened that placed
to be filled with something
designed just for you.

Shadows and Scars (Reprise)

There is rest in this place
where grace abounds,
because not every shadow
haunts me with shame.

In the shadow of Your wings,
all other shadows flee.

There is rest in this love
that never fails,
because not every scar
aches with all I've lost.

In the depth of Your scars,
all other scars find their healing.

Sweet in My Lungs

I have always known
only Your love satisfies this longing –

not a God-shaped hole to be
once filled, always filled,
but lungs, constantly
needing fresh air.

You know me through and through,
keep loving me all the same,
constant without condition,
abundance just a breath away,

but I've kept my mouth shut
as if I could find something else,
gasping between failed attempts,
finding You sweet in my lungs,
forgetting as soon as I exhale.

I want to fall asleep in Your arms,
to settle into a gentle pattern,
my chest rising and falling
to the rhythm of rest in You.

VIII.

I've Seen You With Closed Eyes

The Rib Taken From My Side

Calm at the center of uncertainty,
the winds of waking howling just outside,
she turned to me and hinted.

I, in turn, left no doubt.

She let me
brush the hair from her face,
tuck it behind her ear,
let my hand
linger on her cheek.

She smiled softly
at my touch.

But in the morning
she evaporated with the dew,
not yet ready to stand by my side,
not yet ready to leave
the world I see through closed eyes.

Abigail

Come, lay your gentle hand
upon my violent arm.

May your touch
turn me from destruction,
may your eyes
purge the toxins from my veins,
and may your wisdom
guide my footsteps.

Let me not take for myself
what the Lord has promised to deliver.

ola

For years, you've wandered
in and out of my dreams,
never to be seen by open eyes,
yet always you seem to promise one day
you'll tell me more than your name,
written on the palm of my hand after a decade –
a mystery greater than knowing nothing at all.

I wake, haunted by something
more real than the waking.

To Know and Stay

In a dream, you find me.

I whisper:
Stay with me just a little longer
as we wait for dawn to flood in
and drown the night.

You take my hand.

I tremble, knowing others
have made attempts, fallen away;
knowing it is only you I want.

You read my eyes and say,
I know where you've been.

You're still holding my hand.

The World at My Fingertips

I unfold the world,
spread it out on the table,
wonder where you are.

Inches are miles,
separating us by distances I can't span
with the width of my hand
or the wish of my heart.

You remain hidden
somewhere just beyond my fingertips.

But the world is more than paper
and my love is more than miles.

I will find you,
no matter how long it takes,
no matter how far,
and we will share this world together.

T. Jason Vanderlaan

Vow

Someday, I'll get down on one knee –
promise that my bones will rest next to yours.

IX.

Sand Beneath, Stars Above

When the Sky is Empty, I Feel Far Away

Sitting in the backyard, cool grass
between my fingers, listening
to the midnight symphony: crickets chirping,
bullfrogs echoing across the field.

I'm sure this night is designed to give hope,
but there are as many planes as stars tonight;
the intermittent fireflies try desperately
to make up for the shortage.

I know: the stars do not change
even when hidden by clouds
or obscured by the haze of city lights.

Stars always contain a promise – certainty
and grandeur displayed in their abundance –

though I can't help but wonder
if Abraham ever thought the sky looked less full
than it did when he first went stargazing
with the God of Stars at his side.

T. Jason Vanderlaan

As Fierce as It is Fragile

Hope is not an easy thing
to smother.

It is not an easy bird
to cage.

Not an easy leak
to plug.

Not a lion
to tame.

Hope is
wild.

Before the Story Unfolds

When You first handed me
the rough draft of chapter one –
an outline scribbled on a napkin –
I couldn't see how this story
could possibly have a happy ending.

There were too many plot holes,
unexplained tragedies,
too many villains and
too many journeys on dark nights
up winding paths on precarious cliffs.

I could barely see a chance for chapter two,
let alone a whole novel.

But You were bubbling with enthusiasm
and I couldn't help but smile –
You always write such beautiful stories.

I know You'll turn even this
into one of Your finest masterpieces yet.

The Movement of the Sun Across the Heavens

Seven years will change a man
almost as much as he is changed
by that first glance
from the eyes of the shepherdess.

The sun changes the tone of his skin,
the work, the texture of his hands,
the wait, the strength of his heart.

For better and for worse.

Our Sight is Not Enough

Not all open doors
are meant to be entered.

Not all closed doors
are impossible to pass through.

Sometimes an open door
is the entrance to a prison.

And sometimes a closed door
is simply a wall of Jericho.

T. Jason Vanderlaan

The Duality of Wondering What's Next

Babylon still clings to me,
but with every weary step
I'm shaking the dust from my feet,
watching the lights of that damned place
grow smaller and dimmer.

Sometimes the night fills my soul
with expectant visions of the future,
and other times all I see
is the slow decay of exile's grasping hands.

Is there a darkness too dark
for light to find its way through?

Because sometimes the dawn whispers
silent promises of love that will remain,
and other times I only hear
the distant scream of famine's vacant voice:

Everything you hold will fall away.
All you want will never stay.

As My Lungs Burn (11:11)

Sometimes I almost regret that prayer:
trust, not certainty.

Anticipation and agony, waiting for
fire to fall from the sky,
a small cloud to rise from the sea.

For three and a half years
the heavens were shut
and a famine devastated the land,
but then–

T. Jason Vanderlaan

Not Yet

This is not the part of the movie
where the narrator proudly announces
that they lived happily ever after
as the credits start to roll.

Not yet.

But this is the moment
when the sun breaks over the horizon
and the long night begins to die.

This is the moment
when the battle turns
and we see hope
gleaming in the warrior's eyes.

This is the moment
when we begin to wonder
if maybe despair isn't inevitable,
and maybe there is a chance
for love to bloom again.

But this is not the end.
Not yet.

Mount Constellation

On a mountaintop in Virginia,
I recline under the open sky, watching
the stars emerge, slowly,
one by one, each making its appearance
with significance and meaning,
gradually filling the sky
with order and disarray –
patterns both familiar and foreign.

They unfold
with patience and grace,
revealing plans as indiscernible
as they are clear.

I wonder why
I am not as patient
with my own life.

T. Jason Vanderlaan

When My Eyes Grow Weary Looking for What You Have Promised

I.
Covered in dust and ash, I wait,
but I have waited long enough
to find my doubts again.

How much longer?
How many more wastelands?

You lead and I follow,
but I need to hear again
that this is worth it all.

II.
The ark door slams shut, thunderclap
of wood against wood resounding
in my ears like vindication.

But all around: smug laughter;
and all above: silent, empty skies.

III.
Waiting for Isaac, I forget
to listen as the silence lengthens,
but against all hope, I still hope
that the promise of laughter
will soon burst upon my eager ears.

IV.
I cannot say what comes next
as I wait for dreams to turn to day.

I hang all my hopes upon His words:

My timing, not yours.
My ways, not yours.

But I guarantee:
No one who waits for Me
will ever see My promises fail.

T. Jason Vanderlaan

As Those I Love Join the Great Cloud of Witnesses

One after another, those who deserved
more from this life are laid to rest,
buried on the wandering side of Jordan.

From a distance, they saw
and welcomed promises
that never arrived.

Their longing reached beyond their grasp,
beyond any of our grasps.

Whether or not I gain in this life
all I look forward to, I know
I will one day share in their fulfillment,
in the culmination of every promise
laid upon our hearts – better for the wait,
made perfect as we open our hands together
to receive more than all we ever hoped for.

Those Who Survive the Sword
Will Find Favor in the Desert

Most of our lives spent: waiting
between the dream and the dream come true.

Treacherous, my heavy eyelids envy
the skeletons sleeping in this valley.

A voice, a whisper – maybe just the wind –
bids me steady my stance, keep watch.

This is not my home,
but it is not yet time to leave.

In the moments ahead,
the wind will shift: subtle, almost
imperceptible, yet inescapably real.

Without a doubt,
despite my doubts,
rescue is coming.

I may not see it, hear it,
or feel it, but it is coming.

I will see the Redeemer's mighty arm –
He alone will have done this,
and together, we will all stand in awe
of Him who is both Author and Finisher.

This is as much an invitation
as a declaration: hope for it,
believe it, expect it.

T. Jason Vanderlaan

Out of Sight, Promises on Pause

This is me
with one last drop of oil
trembling on the lip of a jar,
as faith is stretched and strengthened.

This is me
without even a drop of wine,
and nothing left but Your promise
to turn this water into something more.

This is me
waiting for the Dawn from on high
to shine bright with mercy.

Even so, I would rather wade
through the depths of this darkness
with You holding my hand,
than bask in the warmth of light
without You.

The In-Between

I'm burning all my maps,
tearing up these charts.

This is, perhaps,
the most terrifying moment.

Behind, nothing
but sand.
In front, nothing
but sand.

Too far to turn back,
too far ahead to yet see.

All I have is Your silent voice
and Your invisible footprints.

T. Jason Vanderlaan

In Despair, Hope

Walk the desert with the children of Abraham,
as if your journey will never end, but remember:

Every glance at the sky above, a reminder.
Every step on the ground beneath, a guarantee.

When you've finished counting all the stars,
and when you've numbered each grain of sand,
then you will begin to understand
the certainty of My promises.

The Wanderer: A Deeper Hunger

He wanders because I wander. The Incarnation entered my world to be with me, so I would know I am not alone. So I would know that I am known and loved.

Sometimes I still want him to make things happen easier or quicker.

But he doesn't. He just keeps walking next to me. And sometimes *that* is all I want: to be with him, to follow him anywhere, even if we wander forever through endless wastelands.

I am learning to trust him in the light and the shadows, in the healing and the scars. I have found in him the fulfillment of a hunger deeper than I thought possible – every word that comes from his mouth is life to me, because every word is overflowing with a love that has no beginning and no end.

When I rest in such love, I am no longer consumed by the lust to achieve, to gain. I am no longer bent on rushing towards whatever might lay over the horizon.

I slow my pace. Let the love grow.

Acknowledgments

I am very grateful for all who helped make this book possible. To everyone who assisted me financially, who took me in under their roof, fed me, and gave me a bed/couch/floor to sleep on: thank you! Your care made it possible for me to finally put all my energy into finishing this project.

I would also like to thank all the churches I fellowshipped with as I wrote this book. It is a blessing to have worshipped with you all. I am especially indebted to R.E.A.C.H. Philadelphia, who welcomed me into their community and nurtured me with their love and support during a very crucial phase of the writing process.

To my amazing editors: Kayla McAuliffe, Jess Cavallaro, Beth-Anne White, and Matthew Lucio (who is also my official Font Expert and Layout Consultant): thank you for putting up with me, for encouraging and challenging me, and for helping me make this book better than it would have been without you.

Finally, I am eternally grateful to Jesus, my guide and companion in both the writing of this book and all the experiences it embodies. I could ask for nothing better than to have Him at my side, wherever I wander.

About Author

Trained in the dark arts of poetry, T. Jason Vanderlaan has cultivated many time-honored techniques and shady qualities. He is self-serious, self-aggrandizing, self-absorbed, and, most importantly, self-deprecating.

On a side note, he exhibits great affection for words, and is an avid proponent of artistry and creativity.

T. Jason Vanderlaan is also the author of *Unspoken Confessions*, the first book in the *DarkLight* series, which wrestles with sexual addiction, lust, and what it means to pursue purity while dating. More than that, it is an attempt at honesty – we all struggle with flaws of our own and with receiving the grace of God.

Unspoken Confessions is a call to find light in the darkness and to allow God to create a new heart in us as we seek to develop healthy relationships.

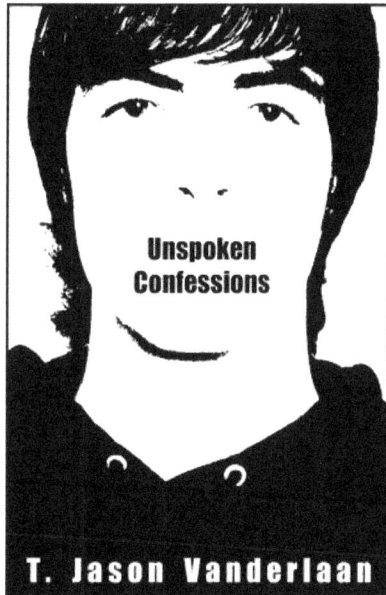

Unspoken Confessions

T. Jason Vanderlaan

Additionally, *Fire* and *Water*, the first two books of Vanderlaan's *Elemental Endeavors* series, are available from Balm and Blade Publishing.

Also available from
Balm and Blade Publishing

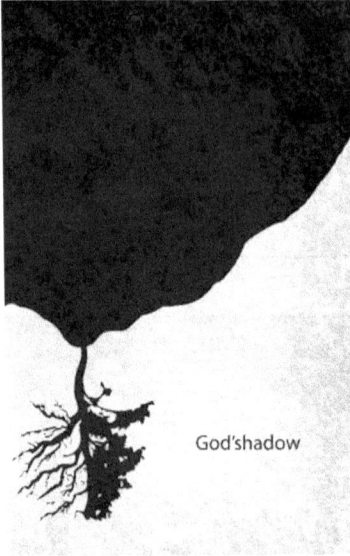

Daniel de Sevén takes us on journey deeper into doubt through a variety of creative essays meant to recall dormant doubts in the reader or else to create new ones. For many it will be an uncomfortable adventure but it is, the author argues, a necessary one because doubt is the delivery room of faith.

But be warned: this book isn't about the author trying to inductively prove a point. Rather, it is at once disjointed and communal, allowing readers to join the discussion and reach their own conclusions.

God'shadow

**For the latest news and updates
from Balm and Blade Publishing,**

**please visit us at:
balmandblade.com
facebook.com/balmandblade**

BALM AND BLADE
PUBLISHING

Chrysalis
BALM AND BLADE PUBLISHING

Chrysalis is a branch of Balm and Blade focused on mentoring new and young authors. By guiding writers through the process of preparing a book for publication, our goal is to help them grow and develop their talents, as well as provide an outlet for them to premiere their creative works.

While our primary focus is on new and young authors, Chrysalis is open to anyone looking for a place to grow and develop the wings of their creativity.

Our first Chrysalis author, John Evans, wrote *Rising From Perdition* during his first three years of high school. Evans draws from his own experiences and dives into the topics of heartache, anger, love, suffering and spirituality. With passion and conviction, he pours his heart out and points us towards the only certainty amidst chaotic flames: Jesus is always with us.

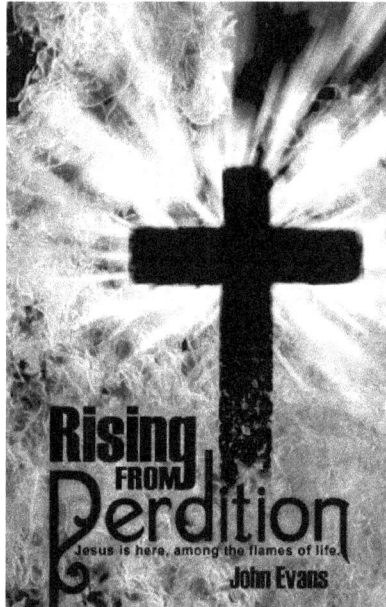

Rising
FROM
Perdition
Jesus is here, among the flames of life.
John Evans

www.ingramcontent.com/pod-product-compliance
Lightning Source LLC
Chambersburg PA
CBHW072006040426
42447CB00009B/1504